FOOTBALL WORLD CUP COMPETITIONS

James Nixon

W
FRANKLIN WATTS
LONDON•SYDNEY

Franklin Watts
First published in Great Britain in 2017 by The Watts Publishing Group

Credits
Editor: James Nixon
Design: Keith Williams, sprout.uk.com
Planning and production by Discovery Books Limited

Photo credits: Cover image: Shutterstock (AGIF).
Getty Images: pp. 5 (Michael Steele /Allsport), 6 bottom (Dean Mouhtaropoulos), 7 top (Popperfoto), 8 (Robert Beck/Sports Illustrated), 10 (Simon Bruty/Allsport), 13 (Simon Bruty /Sports Illustrated), 15 top (JOE KLAMAR/AFP), 17 (Bob Thomas), 22 (Aldo Castillo/LatinContent), 23 (JUAN MABROMATA/AFP), 24 (Mike Hewitt/FIFA), 25 (Shaun Botterill/FIFA), 26 (Paul Gilham), 27 bottom (Popperfoto), 28 top (Ian MacNicol).
Shutterstock: pp. 4 top (AGIF), 4 bottom (Mitch Gunn), 7 bottom (A.RICARDO), 11 top (Marco Iacobucci EPP), 11 bottom (katatonia82), 12 (Lev Radin), 16 top and bottom (A.RICARDO), 18 top (gguy), 18 bottom (Mitch Gunn), 19 top (CosminIftode), 19 bottom (Ververidis Vasilis), 20 (A_Lesik), 21 (katatonia82), 29 top (imagestockdesign), 29 middle (Marco Iacobucci EPP), 29 bottom (Fingerhut).
Wikimedia: pp. 6 top (National Media Museum), 9 top (Nicki Dugan Pogue), 9 bottom (Agência Brasil Fotografias), 14 (Ben Sutherland), 15 bottom (Mustapha Ennaimi), 27 top (Carlos Yo), 28 bottom (joshjdss).

Every attempt has been made to clear copyright. Should there be any inadvertent omission please apply to the publisher for rectification.

ISBN: 978 1 4451 5578 4

Printed in China

Franklin Watts
An imprint of
Hachette Children's Group
Part of The Watts Publishing Group
Carmelite House
50 Victoria Embankment
London EC4Y 0DZ

An Hachette UK Company
www.hachette.co.uk

www.franklinwatts.co.uk

The statistics in this book were correct at the time of printing, but because of the nature of sport, it cannot be guaranteed that they are now accurate.

Every effort has been made by the Publishers to ensure that the websites in this book are suitable for children, that they are of the highest educational value, and that they contain no inappropriate or offensive material. However, because of the nature of the Internet, it is impossible to guarantee that the contents of these sites will not be altered. We strongly advise that Internet access is supervised by a responsible adult.

CONTENTS

UP FOR THE CUP

The ambition of any professional footballer is to win trophies. There are not many better feelings than hoisting a cup into the air in celebration. As well as national **leagues**, there are cup competitions held all over the world to give teams the chance of glory.

It's a knockout

Cup competitions end in exhilarating grand finals, played out in front of tens of thousands of fans, often at big national stadiums. Teams reach a final by winning nerve-jangling **knockout** matches.

Above: Germany won the World Cup in 2014.

Club and country

There are cup competitions for both clubs and countries. The most **prestigious** event is the FIFA World Cup, contested by every footballing nation. National sides also take part in continental cups, such as the European Championships or Asian Cup.

Club sides compete to be crowned national champions in **domestic cups**. The top clubs from each nation also qualify to play in international competitions, such as the UEFA Champions League or Asian Champions League.

Mesut Özil (right) battles for Arsenal in a Champions League match against French side Paris Saint-Germain.

FLASH FACT

The English club with the most wins in domestic and international cup competitions is Liverpool, with 24.

Rise of the underdog

Knockout matches are unpredictable. In a single game anything can happen. It is the perfect chance for an **underdog** to triumph over their stronger opponent. The history of cup football has seen some remarkable shocks.

One of the most stunning cup runs ever came in the 2000 Coupe de France (French Cup). **Amateur** side Calais RUFC included teachers and office workers, but amazingly they reached the final, beating top division clubs Strasbourg and Bordeaux along the way! However, in the final, Calais' dreams were crushed when Nantes scored the winning goal in the last minute to win 2-1.

TALES FROM HISTORY

One of the biggest upsets in World Cup history happened at the 1966 tournament held in England. North Korea became the first team from outside Europe or South America to advance to the **quarter-finals** when they beat two-time world champions Italy 1-0. The Koreans were welcomed back into their country as heroes. The Italian squad stepped off the plane and were pelted with tomatoes and eggs!

Calais fans sing and raise their scarves in the French Cup final in 2000.

THE WORLD CUP

Every four years the most watched sporting event in the world takes place – the FIFA World Cup. Thirty-one national teams from across the globe must **qualify** from **groups** on their continent in order to join the host nation and compete for football's greatest prize.

The tournament begins

The 32 teams that have qualified across six footballing continents are placed into eight groups of four teams. Each group is like a mini-league in which the teams play each other once. The top two teams from each group then advance to the 'last 16' or the 'knockout stage'.

Right: The Queen presents winning captain Bobby Moore with the World Cup trophy after England's World Cup victory in 1966.

Below: Sergio Romero saved two penalties in a shoot-out against The Netherlands to send Argentina through to the World Cup final in 2014.

High drama

In the knockout stage, the drama is high. Teams face each other in a one-off match to decide who is knocked out of the tournament. If the scores are level after **extra time** a **penalty shoot-out** decides the winner. During **penalties** some players crack under the huge pressure, while others become heroes.

Tostao (left) and Pelé celebrate their fourth goal against Italy in the 1970 final.

TALES FROM HISTORY

The Brazilian team crowned champions in the 1970 World Cup hosted by Mexico is often said to be the greatest World Cup team ever. The team contained many skilful stars including perhaps the best player of all time – Pelé. The team had a perfect record – winning all six games in the competition as well as every single qualifier. In the final they thrashed Italy 4-1.

The final

Eventually two teams are left and it is the final. The teams battle for the famous trophy made from 18-carat gold. The match is watched by over one billion people across the globe – about a seventh of the world's population!

Golden prizes

The Golden Boot is awarded to the top scorer in the tournament. The best goalkeeper is given the Golden Glove Award. Frenchman Just Fontaine holds the record for the most goals scored in a World Cup. He netted the ball 13 times in just six games in 1958.

The current World Cup trophy shows two figures holding up the Earth and has been used since 1974.

ROLL OF HONOUR

1930	Uruguay
1934	Italy
1938	Italy
1950	Uruguay
1954	West Germany
1958	Brazil
1962	Brazil
1966	England
1970	Brazil
1974	West Germany
1978	Argentina
1982	Italy
1986	Argentina
1990	West Germany
1994	Brazil
1998	France
2002	Brazil
2006	Italy
2010	Spain
2014	Germany

WOMEN'S WORLD CUP

The FIFA Women's World Cup is also held every four years. The first tournament featured 12 countries and was staged by China in 1991.

Brandi Chastain (bottom-right) and her teammates celebrate as they win the World Cup for the USA in 1999.

TALES FROM HISTORY

The 1999 World Cup was held in the United States and the hosts beat Brazil 2-0 to reach the final. On final day, 90,185 passionate fans packed into the Pasadena Rose Bowl in California to see the US take on China. It remains the largest crowd ever to watch a women's sporting event. After a 0-0 draw, and penalties tied at 4-4, Brandi Chastain had the chance to score the winning penalty. The stadium fell silent … and then erupted with joy as Chastain put the ball into the net. It is the only time the host nation has won the tournament.

Qualifying

Since 2015, 24 teams take part in the World Cup. Qualifiers are held in each of FIFA's six continental zones, such as Europe, Africa and Asia. Each zone has a different number of qualifying spots up for grabs.

Eight teams from Europe are set to join hosts, France, at the 2019 World Cup. The qualifying tournament in Europe sees seven groups of five teams play each other at home and away. The seven group winners will go to the World Cup, while the four best runners-up fight it out in a **play-off** for the final spot.

The United States score in their 5-2 thrashing of Japan in the 2015 World Cup final.

The group stage

At the World Cup finals, the 24 nations are split into six groups of four; the **draw** for the World Cup is carried out months before, but is always an exciting event. The top two sides in each group plus the four best third-place finishers reach the last-16 knockout stage.

Record breakers

Brazilian legend Marta (right) is the all-time leading scorer at World Cups. The five-time World Player of the Year has notched up 15 goals between the 2003 and 2015 tournaments.

At the 2015 World Cup, midfielders Formiga of Brazil and Homare Sawa of Japan made a remarkable record of appearing in six World Cups over a span of 20 years. This feat has never been achieved in men's football.

ROLL OF HONOUR

	1991	1995	1999	2003	2007	2011	2015
United States	Norway	United States	Germany	Germany	Japan	United States

THE EUROS

The UEFA European Championship, often called the Euros, is a competition to be crowned top nation in Europe. It is held every four years, two years before and after a World Cup.

Growing competition

The first European Championship tournament held in France in 1960 was contested by just four nations. It stayed that way until the 1980 Euros expanded to include eight teams and a group stage. Euro 96 held in England doubled the number of teams to 16. Today, 55 countries enter qualifying groups in a bid to become one of 24 nations at the finals.

Past champs

The 15 Euros have been won by ten different national teams. Yet, England's best performance is only a semi-final penalty shoot-out defeat to Germany at Euro 96. The tournament has produced some unexpected results. In 1992 Denmark didn't even qualify, but were invited at the last moment when Yugoslavia were disqualified. They went on to defeat the then world champions, Germany, 2-0 in the final.

Euro 2004 had an even bigger shock. Before the competition, Greece had never won a match at a major tournament. They stunned hosts Portugal in the final, winning the match 1-0.

TALES FROM HISTORY

The 1976 final is known for probably the most famous penalty kick in football history. After extra time, Czechoslovakia and West Germany were tied 2-2, and for the first time the Euros was to be decided by a penalty shoot-out. After West Germany missed, Czechoslovakia's Antonín Panenka had a shot to win the game. Under great pressure, Panenka chose to gently chip the ball towards the middle of the goal. The German goalkeeper had dived early and could only watch the ball drift into the net!

The skilful Brian Laudrup (right) was one of the star players in Denmark's Euro 92 victory.

Superstar Cristiano Ronaldo (right) captained Portugal to European Championship glory in 2016.

Goal getters

Two players are tied with a record nine goals in European Championships. Cristiano Ronaldo has found the net nine times across four different Euros between 2004 and 2016. Three of his goals in 2016 helped Portugal win its first-ever major trophy.

Frenchman Michel Platini scored all of his nine goals in just five matches at Euro 1984! This included two **hat-tricks** in the group stage and a goal to help France beat Spain 2-0 in the final.

ROLL OF HONOUR

1960	1964	1968	1972	1976	1980	1984	1988	1992	1996	2000	2002	2008	2012	2016
Soviet Union	Spain	Italy	West Germany	Czechoslovakia	West Germany	France	Netherlands	Denmark	Germany	France	Greece	Spain	Spain	Portugal

COPA AMERICA

South America has always contained some of the best international sides on the planet. These nations come together at the Copa America tournament every few years, to battle it out to be the best on the continent.

Stat Tracker

	Titles	Runners-up	Third
Uruguay	15	6	9
Argentina	14	14	4
Brazil	8	11	7
Paraguay	2	6	7
Chile	2	4	5
Peru	2	0	8
Colombia	1	1	4
Bolivia	1	1	0
Mexico	0	2	3

Uruguayan striker Edinson Cavani (centre) shoots for goal against Venezuela.

The oldest trophy

The Copa America is the world's oldest international football competition. It was first contested in 1916 between Uruguay, Argentina, Brazil and Chile. Uruguay were the victors and have since won a record 15 titles.

Today, 12 teams compete for the cup. Since 1993, Mexico, a country in Central America, have been invited to play with the ten footballing nations from South America, plus one other team usually from North or Central America. These teams are placed in three groups of four, where eight teams try to qualify for the quarter-finals.

Lionel Messi's magic failed to work for Argentina in the 2016 Copa America final as Chile (in red) won the title.

Chile's charge

Until recently, Chile had never won the Copa America. After nearly 100 years of waiting they have now won the last two trophies. In 2015, as hosts, they beat Argentina in the final in a penalty shoot-out. 2016 was a special 100-year anniversary edition of the tournament and contained 16 teams. Amazingly, history repeated itself in the final. Chile defeated Argentina on penalty kicks after another 0-0 draw. The great Lionel Messi was one of the players to miss!

ROLL OF HONOUR

1993	1995	1997	1999	2001	2004	2007	2011	2015	2016
Argentina	Uruguay	Brazil	Brazil	Colombia	Brazil	Brazil	Uruguay	Chile	Chile

TALES FROM HISTORY

At the 2001 Copa America, the small nation of Honduras were invited to play. Despite arriving at the tournament with barely enough players they pulled off the biggest shock in Copa America history by beating Brazil 2-0 in the quarter-finals. Brazil manager Luiz Felipe Scolari said after the game 'I will go down in history as the Brazil coach who lost to Honduras – it's horrible!' Honduras ended up finishing third while hosts Colombia won their first ever Copa America.

AFRICA CUP OF NATIONS

In 1957, the first Africa Cup of Nations was contested by just three countries – Egypt, Sudan and Ethiopia. Now over 50 teams try to qualify for the 16-team tournament, which is now held every two years.

⚽ Stat Tracker

	Titles	Runners-up	Third
Egypt	7	2	3
Ghana	4	5	1
Cameroon	5	2	1
Nigeria	3	4	7
Ivory Coast	2	2	4
DR Congo	2	0	2
Zambia	1	2	3
Tunisia	1	2	1
Sudan	1	2	1
Algeria	1	1	2
Morocco	1	1	1
Ethiopia	1	1	1
South Africa	1	1	1
Congo	1	0	0

Champions of Africa

Egypt is the most successful nation in the cup's history. They have won a record seven trophies including the first-ever tournament. However, the competition is wide open. In the 31 tournaments there have been 14 different winners. Seven-times finalists Nigeria, nicknamed the Super Eagles, were champions in 2013 but failed to even qualify in 2015 and 2017.

The Ivory Coast triumphed in 2015, winning a marathon penalty shoot-out against Ghana. After every outfield player had taken a penalty, the scores were level at 8-8. Ivorian goalkeeper, Boubacar Barry, then stepped up to be the hero. After saving the Ghana goalkeeper's penalty, he scored himself to win the cup.

Goalkeeper Boubacar Barry scores the winning penalty for the Ivory Coast at the 2015 Africa Cup of Nations.

TALES FROM HISTORY

In 2010 Egypt achieved something that had never been done before. They won their third Africa Cup of Nations in a row. In three finals they had beaten Ivory Coast, Cameroon and Ghana without even conceding a goal! Egypt also set a record for being unbeaten in 19 consecutive Cup of Nations' matches. Incredibly, after this, Egypt failed to qualify for the next three tournaments.

Captain Ahmed Hassan celebrates Egypt's victory in the 2010 Africa Cup of Nations.

Record scorer

The all-time leading scorer in the history of the Africa Cup of Nations is former Barcelona and Chelsea striker Samuel Eto'o (right). Eto'o scored 18 times over six tournaments for Cameroon and helped them lift the trophy twice in 2000 and 2002. He is the most decorated African footballer ever, winning African Footballer of the Year four times in his career. He retired from international football in 2014.

ROLL OF HONOUR

1998	Egypt
2000	Cameroon
2002	Cameroon
2004	Tunisia
2006	Egypt
2008	Egypt
2010	Egypt
2012	Zambia
2013	Nigeria
2015	Ivory Coast
2017	Cameroon

THE OLYMPICS

Every four years male and female footballers take part in the 'greatest show on Earth' – the Olympic Games. Here the players have a chance to take home an Olympic gold medal.

Going pro

Professional players have competed in men's Olympic football since 1984. Today, 16 teams from across the world enter the competition. But there is one big difference from the World Cup. The majority of players must be aged 23 or under. Each squad is allowed to choose just three players over 23.

Captain and over-23 player Neymar wins a gold medal for Brazil in 2016.

ROLL OF HONOUR MEN'S EVENT

1984	1988	1992	1996	2000	2004	2008	2012	2016
France	Soviet Union	Spain	Nigeria	Cameroon	Argentina	Argentina	Mexico	Brazil

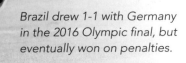

Brazil drew 1-1 with Germany in the 2016 Olympic final, but eventually won on penalties.

16

TALES FROM HISTORY

In 1996 the Nigerian Super Eagles became the first ever African nation to win a world tournament. The speedy and skilful Nigerians faced Argentina in the final. With a minute to go, the score was 2-2 and Nigeria had a free kick just outside Argentina's **penalty box**. The kick was taken and the Argentinian defence stepped up to catch Nigeria **offside**. It didn't work. Daniel Amunike, left all alone, whirled and hammered the ball out of mid-air into the bottom corner of the net. Nigeria had won gold and made history!

Celestine Babayaro (centre) scores Nigeria's first goal in the 1996 Olympic final against Argentina.

Team GB

Great Britain does not normally enter a men's or women's football team at the Olympics. This is because the home nations – England, Scotland, Wales and Northern Ireland – have separate national sides. When London hosted the 2012 Games, the nations joined together to form Team GB. Both the men's and women's teams were knocked out in the quarter-finals.

US golds

Women's football was introduced at the 1996 Olympic Games. Twelve teams qualify and there is no age limit. The United States have been the dominating force in Olympic football, winning four golds and one silver (runners-up medal) out of the six competitions. The 2016 Olympics was the first time they did not win a medal.

ROLL OF HONOUR WOMEN'S EVENT

	1996	2000	2004	2008	2012	2016
	United States	Norway	United States	United States	United States	Germany

CHAMPIONS LEAGUE

The UEFA Champions League is regarded as the greatest competition in club football. It is contested by Europe's top clubs. The tournament's final is the most watched annual sporting event worldwide.

The competitors

Only the very best play in the Champions League. Every European nation's league champion enters. Europe's strongest leagues send their top four sides to the tournament. Thirty-two teams qualify for the league stage either automatically or through **preliminary** knockout rounds.

ROLL OF HONOUR

2007	2008	2009	2010	2011	2012	2013	2014	2015	2016	2017
AC Milan (ITA)	Manchester United (ENG)	Barcelona (SPA)	Inter Milan (ITA)	Barcelona (SPA)	Chelsea (ENG)	Bayern Munich (GER)	Real Madrid (SPA)	Barcelona (SPA)	Real Madrid (SPA)	Real Madrid (SPA)

The league stage

The Champions League used to be called the European Cup. Back then it was a straight knockout competition. Since 1992, the tournament organisers increased the number of teams and added the league stage. The 32 clubs are drawn into eight groups where the teams play their group rivals twice, home and away. The group winners and runners-up advance to the knockout stage.

Chelsea (in blue) in Champions League action against Ukranian champions Dynamo Kyiv in 2015.

Real Madrid's Welsh winger, Gareth Bale, sprints with the ball in the 2016 Champions League semi-final against Manchester City.

Magical Madrid

2017 champions Real Madrid have won more Champions Leagues/European Cups than any other club (12). In fact, from 1956 to 1960 the club won the first five titles, including a record 7-3 thrashing of German club Eintracht Frankfurt in the 1960 final. Spanish clubs have been the most successful with 17 victories, followed by clubs from Italy and England (12 each). Celtic won Scotland's only trophy back in 1967.

TALES FROM HISTORY

Liverpool are England's most successful Champions League club with five victories. Their comeback in the 2005 Champions League final against AC Milan created one of the greatest cup matches ever. At half-time Liverpool were 3-0 down and their dreams looked shattered. Within the space of just six second-half minutes, Liverpool, inspired by captain and Man of the Match Steven Gerrard, sensationally tied the game. AC Milan were stunned and never recovered. They missed three of their penalties in the shoot-out and Liverpool became champions.

Women's champions

The UEFA Women's Champions League was founded in 2001. German clubs have dominated the event, winning nine out of the 15 competitions. FFC Frankfurt have a record four titles. The only British club to triumph so far are Arsenal Ladies in 2007.

KIF Örebro of Sweden (in red) battle with PAOK of Greece in the 2016 Women's Champions League.

EUROPA LEAGUE

The UEFA Europa League is Europe's second biggest cup competition. It contains the best performing sides in Europe's national cups and leagues that didn't qualify for the Champions League.

Two cups become one

In 1960 the UEFA Cup Winners Cup was formed – a contest between all of the European nations' domestic cup winners, such as the FA Cup winners in England. In 1971, the UEFA Cup was also set up for high finishers in Europe's leagues. These two pure knockout competitions merged in 1999. A group stage was added to the UEFA Cup in 2005 and it was renamed the Europa League in 2009.

Zlatan Ibrahimovic (right) competes for Manchester United in the Europa League after the club won the 2016 FA Cup.

Legs and aggregates

The league stage consists of 12 groups. There are four teams in each group that play each other twice. The top two sides in each group progress to the last-32 knockout stage. Here they are joined by the eight clubs that finished third in their Champions League groups.

Before the showpiece final, Champions League and Europa League knockout matches are played over two **legs**, with each side playing home and away. If the **aggregate** score is level, the winner is decided by the number of away goals scored. If away goals are also equal, extra time and penalties are used.

FLASH FACT

Former Celtic and Swedish striker Henrik Larsson holds the record for the most UEFA Cup/Europa League goals. He scored 40 times in 56 games.

	2007	2008	2009	2010	2011	2012	2013	2014	2015	2016	2017
	Sevilla (SPA)	Zenit Saint Petersburg (RUS)	Shakhtar Donetsk (UKR)	Atlético Madrid (SPA)	Porto (POR)	Atlético Madrid (SPA)	Chelsea (ENG)	Sevilla (SPA)	Sevilla (SPA)	Sevilla (SPA)	Manchester United (ENG)

Startling Sevilla

Sevilla from Spain have a phenomenal record in the Europa League. Their record five trophies have all come since 2006. Between 2014 and 2016 Sevilla were unstoppable, winning every title. Three-time winners Liverpool were the victims in the 2016 final. Daniel Sturridge had given Liverpool a half-time lead, but Sevilla still cruised to a 3-1 victory.

British victories

In the very first UEFA Cup in 1972, two English teams reached the final. In those days the final was played over two legs. Tottenham Hotspur beat Wolverhampton Wanderers 3-2 on aggregate. Liverpool, Ipswich Town and Chelsea have also been champions. Scottish clubs have been runners-up three times, most recently Rangers in 2008.

The Sevilla team celebrate with the Europa League trophy in 2015.

Stat Tracker

	Cups per nation	Runners-up per nation
Spain	10	5
Italy	9	6
England	8	6
Germany	6	8
Netherlands	4	3
Portugal	2	5
Sweden	2	0
Russia	2	0
Belgium	1	2
Ukraine	1	1
Turkey	1	0

COPA LIBERTADORES

Outside of Europe, the most prestigious club competition is the Copa Libertadores. It is like the Champions League, but is played every year by clubs in South America.

Since 1998, top clubs from Mexico in Central America have been invited to join the Copa Libertadores. Today, at least the best three clubs from every country enter the tournament. Top nations Argentina and Brazil send five clubs to compete for glory.

ROLL OF HONOUR

2007	2008	2009	2010	2011	2012	2013	2014	2015	2016
Boca Juniors (ARG)	LDU Quito (ECU)	Estudiantes (ARG)	Internacional (BRA)	Santos (BRA)	Corinthians (BRA)	Atlético Mineiro (BRA)	San Lorenzo (ARG)	River Plate (ARG)	Atlético Nacional (COL)

No added time

One of the few differences to the UEFA Champions League is that until the final, extra time is never used. If the aggregate score in a knockout game is equal it goes straight to the dreaded penalty shoot-out.

The American dream

The Copa Libertadores means a lot to the South American fans, and it is a massive part of South American culture. Some players prefer to stay and fight for a Copa Libertadores title despite the lure of a big-money move to Europe. The former Brazilian-born star, Deco, said he would rather swap his two Champions League winners' medals for a Copa Libertadores triumph.

Fans of Atlético Nacional celebrate as their team heads to victory in the 2016 Copa Libertadores final.

POSTOBA

Argentina's River Plate won the 2015 Copa Libertadores, beating Mexican side Tigres 3-0 over two legs.

Top dogs

Since the Copa Libertadores' founding in 1960, Independiente of Argentina have the best record, winning seven titles. However, their last victory was in 1984. Their national rivals, Boca Juniors, are just one behind with six trophies. Ten different Brazilian clubs have won the tournament, but none have won more than three times.

TALES FROM HISTORY

Ecuador-born Alberto Spencer scored 54 goals in 87 Copa Libertadores games between 1960 and 1972. No one has come close to reaching that tally. Spencer was one of the greatest footballers to have lived, yet few have heard of him because he never played in Europe or at a World Cup. He had lethal pace and an extraordinary heading ability. He won three Copa Libertadores titles with Uruguayan side Penarol.

Stat Tracker

	Cups per nation	Runners-up per nation
Argentina	24	9
Brazil	17	15
Uruguay	8	8
Colombia	3	7
Paraguay	3	5
Chile	1	5
Ecuador	1	3
Mexico	0	3
Peru	0	2

CLUB WORLD CUP

Since 2005, a FIFA Club World Cup has been held every December, where one team is crowned club champion of the world.

According to FIFA, the first attempt to create a world championship for clubs was made in 1909. However, the tournament played in Italy was only contested by European clubs. It was nearly a century later, in 2000, before the first truly global Club World Cup took place.

Short knockout

The competition features just seven teams and lasts just over a week. The UEFA Champions League and Copa Libertadores victors, along with each Champions League winner from the other four continents qualify. The seventh team are the winners of the host nation's national league championship.

The European and South American champions receive a **bye** into the semi-final and cannot face each other until the final. This has resulted in most finals pitting Europe against South America. However, two clubs from Africa have managed to reach the final – TP Mazembe from the Democratic Republic of Congo and Raja Casablanca from Morocco.

FLASH FACT

Spanish manager Pep Guardiola is the only manager to win three Club World Cups – twice with Barcelona, and once with Bayern Munich.

Japan hosted the 2016 Club World Cup. Their club Kashima Antlers (in red and black) reached the final but lost 4-2 to Real Madrid.

Brilliant Barcelona

Barcelona hold the record with three Club World Cup triumphs. In 2015 they swept aside Argentinian side River Plate 3-0 in the final. Goal machine Luis Suárez from Uruguay won the Golden Boot, scoring five times in Barcelona's two games!

Three Brazilian clubs have been crowned champions, but Argentina are yet to taste success. Four different Argentinian teams have lost in the final! Manchester United are the only English winners. Wayne Rooney scored the only goal of the final in 2008 against LDU Quito of Ecuador.

Barcelona winners Andrés Iniesta (left) and Luis Suárez pose with the trophy after the 2015 final.

ROLL OF HONOUR

2007	2008	2009	2010	2011	2012	2013	2014	2015	2016
AC Milan (ITA)	Manchester United (ENG)	Barcelona (SPA)	Inter Milan (ITA)	Barcelona (SPA)	Corinthians (BRA)	Bayern Munich (GER)	Real Madrid (SPA)	Barcelona (SPA)	Real Madrid (SPA)

The six pillars

The Club World Cup trophy has six pillars standing on a golden pedestal. These represent the six footballing continents. The pillars hold up a globe that looks like a football.

THE FA CUP

Dating back to 1871, the FA Cup for English clubs is the oldest competition in the world. Clubs fight their way through thrilling knockout matches to reach the final at Wembley Stadium. There are no groups, no second legs, and no second chances if you lose!

Non-league teams

The FA Cup is unique. All **non-league** clubs, including those that are not fully professional, have the chance to qualify. Around 750 clubs enter the tournament each year! After six qualifying rounds, **League 1** and **League 2** clubs join the qualifiers in the first-round proper. In the third round, Premier League and **Championship** teams, containing the big clubs, start their quest for glory.

Manchester United beat Crystal Palace 2-1 in the 2016 FA Cup final to win their 12th title.

The draw

The draw for the third round is tense and exciting. Non-league clubs that have made it this far wait to see if they get paired with a Premier League giant, such as Manchester United. Most teams are looking for a home **fixture** to give themselves an advantage.

Before the quarter-final stage, matches that end in a draw go to a replay. In the replay, the away team now gets the chance to play at home. If the match is tied again, extra time and penalties can be used.

Giant killers

The FA Cup has produced many memorable **giant killings**. In 1992, Wrexham had just finished bottom of England's fourth division of football, yet they dumped league champions Arsenal out of the cup with two late goals in a 2-1 win. The fans went delirious and invaded the pitch.

In 2017, underdogs Lincoln City and Sutton United reached the fifth round. It was the first time that two non-league sides had reached the last 16 since 1888. Lincoln City then shocked Premier League Burnley, winning 1-0, and became the first non-league team to appear in the quarter-finals for 103 years!

FLASH FACT

Yeovil Town hold the record with 20 league giant killings as a non-league team.

TALES FROM HISTORY

Blackpool's 4-3 defeat of Bolton Wanderers in 1953 is one of the most famous FA Cup finals. Blackpool's side featured star winger Stanley Matthews (right), who later became the first footballer to be knighted. Matthews was 38, and with Bolton 3-1 up in the second half, his chance of an FA Cup winner's medal looked to be fading. But then Matthews put in the performance of his life. His dazzling dribbling skills spurred Blackpool on to a last-minute victory. The final became known as the 'Matthews Final' despite teammate Stan Mortensen scoring a hat-trick!

27

NATIONAL CUPS

Most countries have a knockout cup competition alongside their national league. Here are some famous national cups:

ROLL OF HONOUR

	2012	2013	2014	2015	2016	2017
	Hearts	Celtic	St Johnstone	Inverness Caledonian Thistle	Hibernian	Celtic

Scottish Cup

The Scottish Cup is the second oldest competition in football history after the FA Cup. The solid-silver trophy is the oldest trophy in the world and has been presented to the winners since 1874. Hampden Park in Glasgow has hosted most of the finals.

Celtic and Rangers have won the majority of finals with 37 and 33 wins respectively. The 2016 final was the first time that it was contested between two clubs from the second **division** of Scottish football. Hibernian beat Rangers with an injury-time goal from captain David Gray (left) to win their first Scottish Cup for 114 years!

ROLL OF HONOUR

	2012	2013	2014	2015	2016	2017
	Birmingham City	Arsenal	Arsenal	Chelsea	Arsenal	Manchester City

Women's FA Cup

The first Women's FA Cup in England was contested in 1971. It was called the Mitre Trophy until the FA took over the running of women's football in 1993. The 2016 champions, Arsenal, are by far the most successful team in the competition's history. Since 1993 they have won 14 titles!

Arsenal Ladies beat Chelsea 1-0 in the 2016 FA Cup final.

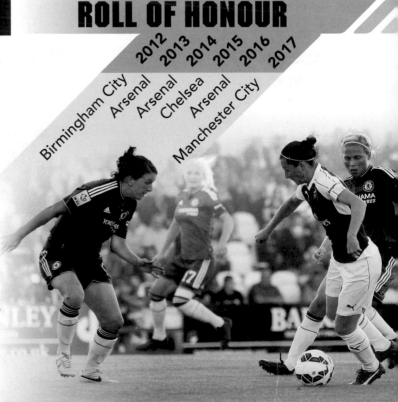

ROLL OF HONOUR

2012	2013	2014	2015	2016	2017
Barcelona	Atlético Madrid	Real Madrid	Barcelona	Barcelona	Barcelona

Neymar (right) runs on to the ball for Barcelona in a Copa Del Rey contest against Atlético Madrid.

Copa Del Rey

The Copa Del Rey is the annual cup for Spanish football teams, played since 1903. The early rounds are single games with lower division teams given the home advantage. When La Liga (top division) teams enter, matches are played over two legs until the final. Barcelona, the 2017 champions, have a record 29 wins.

Coppa Italia

The Italian Cup (Coppa Italia) was first held in 1922 and has been contested every year since 1958. The draw for the whole competition is made before a ball is kicked. Matches are single legs apart from a two-legged semi-final. Juventus achieved a league and cup triple in 2015, 2016 and 2017 and have the most cup victories with 12.

ROLL OF HONOUR

2012	2013	2014	2015	2016	2017
Napoli	Lazio	Napoli	Juventus	Juventus	Juventus

Left: Juventus players celebrate after victory against AC Milan in 2016.

DFB Pokal

The German knockout cup is called the DFB Pokal and was founded in 1935. Giants Bayern Munich have won a record 18 times. Sixty-four teams start the competition. In the first round, top-flight sides are matched against amateur teams. This has led to some massive surprises. TSV Vestenbergsgreuth, based in a small village of just 6,000 people, upset Bayern Munich 1-0 in 1994!

ROLL OF HONOUR

2012	2013	2014	2015	2016	2017
Borussia Dortmund	Bayern Munich	Bayern Munich	Wolfsburg	Bayern Munich	Borussia Dortmund

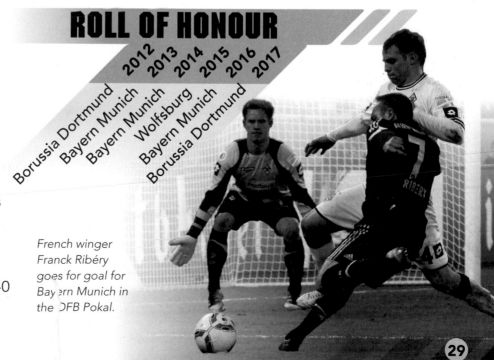

French winger Franck Ribéry goes for goal for Bayern Munich in the DFB Pokal.

GLOSSARY

aggregate the total score between two teams that have played two legs or more

amateur non-professional

bye a free passage into the next round of a competition without having to play a game

Championship the second highest division in English football

division a group of teams joined together for a league competition

domestic cup a cup competition contested by football clubs in just one country

draw when teams are selected at random to see which sides will face each other in a competition

extra time thirty added minutes when the score is tied after ninety minutes

fixture a match scheduled to take place on a particular date

giant killing when an underdog beats a top-flight team

group a mini-league in which the winners advance to the next stage of a competition

hat-trick the scoring of three goals in one game by one player

knockout a tournament in which the losers at each stage are eliminated

league a competition in which a group of teams play each other for points over a set period

League 1 the third highest division in English football

League 2 the fourth highest division in English football

legs the matches played between two clubs that decide which team advances to the next stage of a competition

non-league describes a team from outside the top four divisions of English football

offside a position on the field where a player cannot be passed the ball. To be onside, players must have two opponents between themselves and the opponent's goal.

penalty a free shot from the penalty spot (11 metres from goal) with just the goalkeeper to beat

penalty box the large rectangular area at each end of the pitch where the goalkeeper can handle the ball

penalty shoot-out a contest where each side takes at least five penalties to decide the outcome of a match

play-off an extra knockout match to decide the outcome of a competition

preliminary an early round of a competition before the main part of that competition starts

prestigious widely celebrated and glamorous

qualify perform well enough to reach the next stage of a competition

quarter-finals the round of a knockout competition that contains the remaining eight teams. It precedes the semi-finals.

underdog a team thought to have little chance of winning

FURTHER INFORMATION

BOOKS

An Infographic Guide to: Football,
Wayland, 2016

Champions League Fact File,
Clive Gifford, Carlton Kids, 2015

The Football Encyclopedia,
Clive Gifford, Kingfisher, 2016

World Cup Expert series,
Pete May, Franklin Watts, 2017

WEBSITES

www.fifa.com/worldcup
The latest World Cup news and results
on the FIFA website.

www.myfootballfacts.com
This site contains a mountain of
stats, including past cup champions
and top goalscorers.

www.thefa.com/competitions/thefacup/
more/history
A history of the FA Cup.

www.uefa.com
News, stats and history for every
UEFA European competition.

INDEX

FOOTBALL WORLD

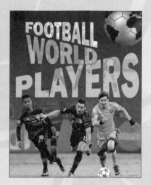

PLAYERS
Stars of the game
Skill players
Pure goalscorers
Targetmen
Number tens
Tricky wingers
Pass masters
Midfield destroyers
Flying full backs
Top defenders
Goalkeepers
Women's football
Stars of the future

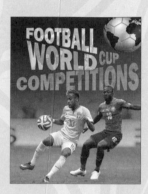

CUP COMPETITIONS
Up for the cup
The World Cup
Women's World Cup
The Euros
Copa America
Africa Cup of Nations
The Olympics
Champions League
Europa League
Copa Libertadores
Club World Cup
The FA Cup
National cups

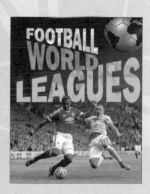

LEAGUES
The global game
The Premier League
The Championship
FA Women's Super League
Scottish Premiership
La Liga
Bundesliga
Serie A
Ligue 1
More Euro leagues
Major League Soccer
National Women's Soccer League
The Brasileirão

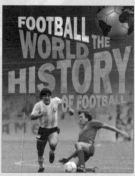

THE HISTORY OF FOOTBALL
In the beginning
The birth of the FA
The laws of the game
The world game
European challenge
Brazil's golden era
British glory
Women's football
Total football
Triumph and tragedy
A new dawn
The rise of France
Spanish dominance